Wild About
Dragsters

J. Poolos

PowerKiDS
press.
New York

Published in 2008 by The Rosen Publishing Group, Inc.
29 East 21st Street, New York, NY 10010

First Edition

Editor: Amelie von Zumbusch
Book Design: Greg Tucker
Photo Researcher: Nicole Pristash

Photo Credits: Cover, pp. 7, 11, 13, 15, 19 © Getty Images; pp. 5, 9, 17, 21 © Shutterstock.com.

Library of Congress Cataloging-in-Publication Data

Poolos, Jamie.
  Wild about dragsters / J. Poolos. — 1st ed.
      p. cm. — (Wild rides)
  Includes bibliographical references and index.
  ISBN-13: 978-1-4042-3792-6 (library binding)
  ISBN-10: 1-4042-3792-5 (library binding)
  1. Dragsters—Juvenile literature. 2. Drag racing—Juvenile literature. I. Title.
  TL236.2.P66 2008
  629.228—dc22
                                              2007000921

Manufactured in the United States of America

Contents

What Is a Dragster?

Dragsters are cars that are used in drag races. In a drag race, two cars or motorcycles race down a straight track to the finish line. Dragsters are built to go fast. They have big, powerful **engines** and fat back tires. These tires give dragsters extra **traction**.

Dragsters leave the race's starting line in a cloud of tire smoke. They scream across the finish line 5 to 10 seconds later. Dragsters go so fast that they need **parachutes** to slow down. There are many kinds of dragsters. Top **fuel** dragsters and funny cars are two of the fastest kinds of dragsters.

This dragster is a top fuel dragster. These are the fastest kind of dragster.

5

How to Spot
a Top Fuel Dragster

Top fuel dragsters are long, thin cars with small, narrow front wheels. These cars sit only 2 to 3 inches (5-8 cm) off the ground. They have powerful engines that make more than 5,500 **horsepower**. The cars have a giant wing at the back to help keep them on the track. All top fuel dragsters must weigh at least 2,225 pounds (1,009 kg).

Top fuel dragsters are the fastest of all dragsters. They rip through ¼ mile (.4 km) in 4.45 seconds and can go faster than 330 miles per hour (531 km/h)!

This top fuel dragster is racing at the Las Vegas Motor Speedway in Las Vegas, Nevada.

How to Spot a Funny Car

One way to tell funny cars and top fuel dragsters apart is that only funny cars have roofs and **windshields**. Funny cars' back wheels are big and wide. Their front wheels are small and narrow. The sets of wheels are always between 124 and 125 inches (315–318 cm) apart.

Funny cars are slower than top fuel dragsters. However, they are still fast! Funny cars have powerful engines that make between 350 and 1,000 horsepower. They can run ¼ mile (.4 km) in under 4.8 seconds. They can go up to 320 miles per hour (515 km/h).

To enter a race, funny cars must weigh at least 2,400 pounds (1,089 kg), with the driver.

Engines and Fuels

Most dragsters have engines called V6 or V8 engines. These engines make between 120 and 5,500 horsepower. **Mechanics** sometimes change these engines to make them more powerful. One way to make a dragster go faster is to add a supercharger or turbocharger. These parts force more air into the engine. This lets the engine burn more fuel and go faster.

Most dragster engines burn high-powered gas. Some use **alcohol**. The fastest dragsters are top fuel dragsters. They burn an **explosive** fuel called **nitromethane**, which makes the cars go extrafast.

The nitromethane fuel that top fuel dragsters use causes them to let off a cloud of smoke and light.

The History of Drag Racing

Organized drag racing began in 1947, when racer Wally Parks helped form the Southern California Timing Association. This group's first races were held at the Bonneville Salt Flats in 1949. This was the first time dragsters raced against a stopwatch. The first real drag strip, or track, was the Santa Ana Drags. It opened in 1950.

In 1951, Parks founded the National Hot Rod Association, or NHRA, to make classes and safety rules for different kinds of cars. Drag racing grew quickly, and today the NHRA is the world's largest motor-sports body, with more than 80,000 members and 140 tracks.

This early dragster came from Bristol, Tennessee. It raced at the Charlestown Naval Air Station, in Rhode Island, in the 1950s.

What Happens at a Drag Race?

Drag races take place on a track that is either ⅛ mile (.2 km) or ¼ mile (.4 km) long. Dragsters are put into classes based on the type of car they are and how quickly they are likely to go. This way, dragsters race only against other dragsters that are about the same size and have the same kind of engine.

When a car wins a race, it races against another winning dragster. The car that loses is done racing for the weekend. The winner of all the races takes home money and a prize called a trophy.

Drag racers are belted in during a drag race. They wear hard hats, called helmets, to keep their heads safe.

The Race Is On!

A drag race happens in a blast of power and noise. It begins when two dragsters back into a puddle, called the waterbox, to wet their back tires. The drivers spin the tires in a **burnout** to get better traction.

When the starting lights turn green, the cars are off in a roar and a cloud of smoke! The drivers change **gears** many times throughout the short race. The fastest dragsters cross the finish line in just 5 seconds! After crossing the finish line, drivers slow down by letting out their parachutes and braking their cars.

These two dragsters are racing against each other at an important race called the NHRA Nationals.

Famous Drag Racers

The most famous drag racer is "Big Daddy" Don Garlits. His top fuel dragster was named Swamp Rat. Garlits was a fast racer who made the sport safer, too. Dragster engines were at the car's front until 1970. That year Garlits lost half his right foot when his dragster's engine blew up. Garlits then built the first dragster with an engine in the back. Today's dragsters have engines in the back. They are safer than the old dragsters.

Funny car racers Don "the Snake" Prudhomme and Tom "the Mongoose" McEwen were **rivals** in the 1960s and 1970s. They helped make the sport **popular**.

Don Garlits is shown here at the NHRA Winter National Drag Racing Championships in 1991.

Pro Stock Cars and Motorcycles

Top fuel dragsters and funny cars are popular, but they are not the only kinds of dragsters. Pro Stock dragsters are drag racers that look like everyday cars. However, Pro Stock cars have more powerful engines than everyday cars. Pro Stock cars can go as fast as 215 miles per hour (346 km/h).

There are also Pro Stock motorcycles that drag race. These motorcycles have engines that make 300 horsepower. They have long bars on them called wheelie bars, which keep them from flipping over. Pro Stock motorcycles can reach almost 200 miles per hour (322 km/h).

Pro Stock motorcycles have bars called wheelie bars that reach out past their back wheel. Wheelie bars keep motorcycles from tipping over.

21

Tomorrow's Dragsters

More and more people try drag racing every year. The NHRA now has more than 35,000 drivers. One of the great things about drag racing is that anyone who can drive can take a car to a club race and give it a try. Some clubs have "midnight madness" drag races that offer a safe place for street racers to run their cars.

Drag racing captivates drivers and fans alike. Over time, dragsters have gotten faster and faster. As the race for lower times continues, look for even more powerful engines in superfast cars. Drag racing is on the move!

Glossary

alcohol (AL-kuh-hol) A clear fuel that pours and burns easily.

burnout (BURN-owt) Spinning a car's back tires in water to clean and heat them.

engines (EN-jinz) Machines inside a car or airplane that make the car or airplane move.

explosive (ek-SPLOH-siv) Something that can blow up.

fuel (FYOOL) Something used to make warmth or power.

gears (GEERZ) Parts of a machine that help it work.

horsepower (HORS-pow-er) The way an engine's power is measured.

mechanics (mih-KA-niks) People who are skilled at fixing machines.

nitromethane (ny-troh-MEH-thayn) A powerful, explosive fuel burned by top fuel dragsters.

organized (OR-guh-nyzd) Well-ordered and planned out ahead of time.

parachutes (PAR-uh-shoots) Large pieces of cloth that are let out, fill with air, and slow something down.

popular (PAH-pyuh-lur) Liked by lots of people.

rivals (RY-vulz) People who try to be as good at or better than each other.

traction (TRAK-shun) The hold a moving object has on a road.

windshields (WIND-sheeldz) Sheets of glass that go across the front of a car, truck, plane, or boat.

Index

A
alcohol, 10

B
Bonneville Salt Flats, 12

D
drivers, 16, 22

G
gears, 16

M
mechanics, 10

N
NHRA, 12, 22
nitromethane, 10

P
parachutes, 4, 16

R
rivals, 18
roofs, 8

S
Santa Ana Drags, 12
supercharger, 10
Swamp Rat, 18

T
tire(s), 4, 16
traction, 4, 16
trophy, 14

W
wheelie bars, 20
windshields, 8

Web Sites

Due to the changing nature of Internet links, PowerKids Press has developed an online list of Web sites related to the subject of this book. This site is updated regularly. Please use this link to access the list: www.powerkidslinks.com/wild/drag/